Leaves Falling Backwards

Heart Attack Poems   Before & After

poems by

Tish Pearlman

Finishing Line Press
Georgetown, Kentucky

Leaves Falling Backwards

Heart Attack Poems   Before & After

Copyright © 2024 by Tish Pearlman
ISBN 979-8-88838-515-9 First Edition
All rights reserved under International and Pan-American Copyright Conventions. No part of this book may be reproduced in any manner whatsoever without written permission from the publisher, except in the case of brief quotations embodied in critical articles and reviews.

ACKNOWLEDGMENTS

Some of these poems appeared in the 2018 & 2019 *Healing Muse Literary Journal*

ALSO BY TISH PEARLMAN

The Fix Is In (Finishing Line Press 2012)
Afterlife (Foothills 2014)

Publisher: Leah Huete de Maines
Editor: Christen Kincaid
Cover Art and Design: ("Through the Woods & Into the Sea") by Treacy Ziegler,
    http://www.treacyzieglerfineart.com
Painting on page 21 (Broken Heart) by Barbara Mink, http://www.barbaramink.com/
Author Photo: Sheryl Sincow

Order online: www.finishinglinepress.com
    also available on amazon.com

> Author inquiries and mail orders:
> Finishing Line Press
> PO Box 1626
> Georgetown, Kentucky 40324
> USA

Contents

Preface xi
Fading Light xv

Before

Forced Entry 1
Remembering 2
Riding Winter 3
Prelude 4
Circling 5
Prayer 6
Playing Tag 7
Old Traveler 8
Into Thin Air 9
Last Breath 10
Ghost 11
Being Born 12
The Return 13
Rooted 14
Upon Entry 15

After

Re-enacting the Beginning 21
Path 22
Requiem 24
I Might Return 25
Still, The Song 26
Forever Now 27
Mirror 28
Singing 29
Farewell 30
Strolling Away 31
Passage 32
Found 33
No Way Home 34

That Other Self	35
The Reveal	36
Last Prayer	37
Retreating	38
Points of Light	39
What is Left	40
Saved	41
Sleep Walking	42
Liftoff	43
The Pageant	44
Launch	45
Seeing	46
Rip-Tide Moon	47
The Circle Opens	48
Launching Again	49
Walking the Path	50
Here Now	51
The Mood of Endings	52
Vanishing Point	54
Whiplash	55
The Scope of Endings	56
Path from Home	57
Reawakened	59
Moored Nowhere	60
The Light Dreams On	61
Fortune	62
Passing	63
Staircase	64
The Path at Last	65
Intruding	66
I'm Here	67
Uneven Path	68
Remaining Present	69
The Ghost Travels	70
The Moment of Faith in Freefall	71
Underneath and	72
To the Shoreline	73
Found Again	74
Meeting the Tides	75
Bleeding	76
Left	77

For Carol J. Painter & John M. Pearlman
And to all of our magnificent friends & family who helped us
Through this nightmare:
Barbara Aburnich, Dick Pearlman, Barbara Mink, Jeanne Mackin,
Joe Laquatra, Johnny Svensson, Helen Gibson, Barbara Warland,
Susan & Steve Pond, Seth & Rebekkah Brahler, Sally & Jerry Sincock,
David & Maree Benedict, Catherine Cannariato, MD, Lynn Swisher, MD

Preface

On December 28, 2017 I was having a holiday drink with my partner and her friend. Around 6pm, I got up, went into the bathroom, and when I came out I told them "something's not right" pointing to my upper chest. Shortly thereafter, I fell back in my chair. My eyes were rolling and I lost consciousness. My partner called 911.

I had a massive heart attack at age 64.

My family was told that I probably would not survive this event. I was in the hospital for over two weeks. I was mentally out of it much of that time. When I went home, I was in a fog for several months: felt like people were coming at me and the walls were closing in. Was paranoid, and my memory had vanished. It took many, many months for me to begin to feel normal.

****

The Day of the heart attack.

December 28, 2017

Fading Light

It could come from pale blue
Sky.
The end, I mean.
You ache to know what
You were meant to
Live for.
The truth rarely unfolds
Like a scroll…
Perhaps for those who
Shun the world, and
Are god bound
The child longs only
To live, but it is
Never enough.
Accept gifts.
Is breath a gift?
Is fear?
We just can't figure
Out which star is ours.
Discover your inhale
& exhale as a
Song. It creates a
Melody.
Face it, you have
Been cast out like
The blue moon:
Beautiful, fleeting and
Unnoticed until you
Locate the heart.

12.28.17

Part One

Before

Forced Entry

The afternoon when I
Was born
Did not last long.
Granted, it was very close
To the longest day of the year…
The Rosenberg's executed bodies were not yet
Cool, the war in Korea…
My first ride may have
Been in a Ford, flying down Highway 1.
The ocean right there, now
In my blood.
They tried to communicate
By calling me a name I could not fathom: Patricia.
That must have silenced me.
   *

When you learn to walk
Are you heading away or
Toward?
I was tiny when I
Arrived.
Maybe because I
Could hide easily
I found a loud voice.
I don't have to practice
Being a human being
I just start by moving into the distance.

1.1.17

Remembering

I await my return as
A tree in
Starlight,
As a child in August.
I await my first
Glimpse of you
All those years
After you died.
I await, still, my
Awakening in a
Small room
Filled with flame.
Her rising still enacted
Over and over
I await those days
When we had quiet
Conversation
You were alone then
The family surrounding
Your exhausted
Spirit
It kept you alive
It kept you alive
We still reside there
In the deep fog of
The coastline
Now, only now we are
Surfacing in snow light,
Enraptured by winter

1.24.17

Riding Winter

We
Have gone north.
Quietly, we had snow
Last night
And that's when the
Night began
Your ashes are now
Roaming the Pacific…
Not a bad ending, ending
There.
Funny how
An entire life vanishes
Into shimmering waves.
No
Hard labor
Only a eulogy
And then you are through
To the wind.
Further along,
There are people fighting
To stay alive
They no longer recognize
The harbor in the night sky.
We will all meet again
So the saying goes
We will have a lot to
Navigate.
Before I wake up and
Find myself in your
Company again
I wish to tell you one
 Little lie:
I learned that counting down
The days is a waste of
Time.
Quietly, maybe on a winter night like this
You merely lean into your life, and your life
Will exhale one last time.

1.28.17

Prelude

I cannot yet imagine
What is dislodging inside
Of me.
Are the stars already
Here?

2.15.17

Circling *(A Meditation)*

And if I should die
while fully awake
will I then become
the dream?
And if I should awaken
in my last breath
will I then become
 the spirit?
And if I am stilled and
my world black as black
will I still meet
the distant stars?
And if I should find,
in this new land
the meaning, the
answers, the truest reasons
for why I walked the earth,
will there be
not a soul to tell?
And if I should return
as a radiant, recognizable
self, beginning all over
again
shall I set out
early
for the road that never ends?

6.12-13.17

Prayer

Even when riding the
Waves
I was homesick for the
Sea.
What was missing was the
Submergence with god.
My church had no
Closed sky…
Instead, the
Night, the night filled
My restless soul as I
Questioned
All of the wide
Awake stars.

8.12.17

Playing Tag

That was the world
Once.
That was climbing crumbling
Walls, settling on the
Roof as the evening awakened.
Running down the
Sand dunes.
That world never
Died. We all lived then.
We all lived in
The same rooms,
We all ran to the
Same shoreline,
We drove the narrow foggy
Coast.
I loved it once,
I loved the going,
The going…
And the dream of reaching.
I am almost done now. I'll meet you
At the last shadow before
Sunrise.

8.26.17

Old Traveler

Is the future being
Convened in this
Room as we go
On with our lives?
The old woman sitting up
In her bed sees it is
Now spring outside her
Window.
She Doses off.
She senses a new season…
When she opens her mind
She knows there is little
Time to apprehend what
Was written in her imaginary journal.
It has all been
Decided and she has
Only today.
What would happen if she
Set her alarm
For darkest night when
You must believe long
Distances will bring
Scattering stars?
She knocks on the door
Of the future.
It is silent on the other
Side, hollowed out, no
Echo.
She is on her own, and
She knows all she needs
To lead the way is
Her opened eyes.

10.29.17

Into Thin Air

What is it like to know
You are very close to
The end?
Each utterance a gift
And the last…
And the last…
Cannot warn you
In the here and now.
The last will be
Forever reinventing,
Sent on in the wake
Of a moment you will
Never meet.

10.7.17

Last Breath

Perhaps the pupils dilate to
Wide open darkness upon death
Because you don't need light
To know the way.

11.5.17

Ghost

It is difficult to know
What is put out in
The world
Because the heart
Is infinite.
The little puffs of breath
Disappear but someone
Saw,
Someone sensed.
The whisper "I am here"
"I am here" dissipates
But will return as dew
In early spring.
The traveler has no destination,
She is merely a shadow
Someone sensed was
Passing.

11.16.17

Being Born

Perhaps there was a
Disturbance or a panic,
Perhaps stress induced
My arrival
Eleven days early.
If I had stayed in the
Warm, dark womb perhaps
I would have been a
Painter or I would have relaxed
In the imagery of the pacific.
I was hurried by a crack
In the velocity of currents.
I was eager to see what becomes of
Spirit when it is unleashed.

11.20.17

The Return

I am aware of the ghost
Tapping around inside me.
Formed from mineral
And constellations
Shadows and
Muted sounds.
But, there was always an
Inkling the sea had been home.
The heart can only take
You so far, the rest is
Disruption.
What have you seen as the
World handed you just so
Many years of keeping watch?
Caught in a circle, there
Is no up or down, there is
Only the return.

12.9.17

Rooted

When I ignite the
Place where seeds conspire
Skyward
No right, no wrong
Only afternoon dissolving,
Perhaps a little rain
And then boundless…
Tied to soil, interrupted
By seasons
When I return to the
Place where beginnings
End with the first glimpse of
Sunlight
I will know what it is
I have loved.

12.12.17

Upon Entry

(For Carol Painter & John Pearlman)

When I finally depart
The sun will still rise,
The moon will note
Solstice, the stars
Will still awaken in
Their dark city.
When I go I will
Know you are awakening
To my first light,
You will know my voice
Has left words
Without shadows
The drifting mind of
My absence melds so
Closely to your memories-
I will not abandon you
I will still be the breeze,
The winter snow fall,
I will still remember you
Calling to me
No voyage is without
Farewell
So, I have emptied
My soul,
The glitter of my light
It's all there for you.

12.17.17

Part II

After

Reenacting the beginning

You no longer live
In this world.
How does one travel
So far with no words,
And then resume the
Memories of sea, of
Laughter, of ministry?
The night rose inside
 you as you changed
Into a limp, oxygen-
Deprived animal.
The contours of a mind
Alive and flowing out of
You like a bleeding wound.
When you began to
Tumble back, to breathe
In the scent of your
Dreaming self…
There it was, a moment
Bordering on blinding.
The wires of the
Nerves still enacting
A steady, burning connection.
There was no thought
Of another morning.
You rose but the
Sun did not.
Believe, believe,
Believe…
The ghost
Was so beautiful
But you returned
Unsteady,
Eating the light.

1.18.18

Path

It is March and it is winter.
When I stare out on the
Snowy landscape if I
Look far enough into fugue
I will be a young girl
Just returned from a
Day at the beach,
Getting excited about
A BBQ in the backyard…
My skin will be red, shoulders,
Face, back. I will feel free
When I snap back from
My long distance away,
I will see I am still
Looming but no longer
In the past.
The day I see now
Resembles a quiet mind.
When did the children's
Voices fade out,
When did the sand hill
Disappear?
Is my mother still waiting
For us to return from
School?
My oldest brothers are
Gone, they are already
Filing their reports from adulthood.
Still, one can forever
Wonder how we all
Ended up there, who
Brought us there.
Did we know there was
Always a road leading out?
I lived for a time
In the attic, my nest,
My mousehole. I could
Hoist up the stair case
And no one could

Reach me.
How strange, a young
girl living like an
old lady in an attic.
My life with my family
Far away. The TV blaring
Game shows. The neighborhood
Sounds; basketball, children's
Voices yelling. Mother's calling "Dinner."
So far away from
My secret hideout.
The future sent me
Across the seas,
All the while
No place really-
Stumble into this world
Grab for that, float, always freedom.
The ghost of the California
Coast…
She learned to fly
Like those before her
but she could not find
a concrete world.
Strong headwinds,
dreaming the roads,
travelling the roads…
Freedom again, so close now.

3.12.18

Requiem

There is no such thing
As a return from
Near death. I am changed
Beyond recognition; *inside,*
Where life began.
I am no longer a viable human being
But a ghost in the world…
I sit and I wait for the
The hour of the dying
Heart, when the
Energy of a lifetime
Meets again with the sea.

5.22.18

I Might Return

There was always a
Will back but no one
Imagined she'd find the
Entryway.
There was help but
No hope.
Alone, awaiting the sign,
The desire
She stumbled into a
New diminished return.
The spring light has
Welcomed her but she
Is baffled (as are her
friends and family) by the
New landscape and the
Body ready for retreat,
Not resurrection.
Both life and death
Call to her. She cannot
Yet let go of the
Memory of waves,
Smiling faces, the
Love.
She found the place
Where absence is
A warm beginning.
Then she is born.

5.22.18

Still, The Song

When she was declared
Dead by drowning in her
Own currents, and her reckless
Heart, she laughed. Did
They respond? Dizzying for
All. Then she is ordered to
Wake up if she can (god is humorous).
Something was left watching
Some spirit of disruption, some
Voice calling frantically.
She stepped aside while
They dreamed her back,
Her life hanging by
A thread. She disappoints
The savior's because she
Is baffled by the bright
Flashes of color.
And the voices talking
All at once.
And the humming of machines.
And, beside it all? She
Mis-placed the spark of
Illumination. Instead, she
Is startled by morning
Retrieved. She is stunned in the
New light-scape, and the
Language is unrecognizable.
She no longer feels poetry, but
She is aroused by beautiful words:
This Is Life.

5.28.18

Forever Now

(For CJP)

When I die you
cannot follow me.
You are not ready
for the blinding light,
the breath of early winter
snowfall, my calling to you.
But when I die you
will remember me.
We have travelled so far from
the abandoned years.
You must follow closely behind now
So that when you pass the rest of
Your life
You will find me there.

6.3.18

Mirror

Mostly it was time passing
To bring her home.
She awoke in the chaotic
Desert of her catastrophe-
Spirit was already in exile…
When she came
Back, she was unafraid
Of living or dying…
What was left is
A self in pieces, but a mind
Intact, because the
Heavens are caring
For her wide-awake
Soul.

6.12.18

Singing

I will go quietly when
I retreat.
As all drift from my
Last words, I will
Not make a sound.
Everything has been
Spoken.
Now it must
Be reconfigured, as memory.
When did I last
Swim the Pacific?
I will go back…
I will go back…
There is such a
Beautiful song along
The shores of my dying
Body.

6.13.18

Farewell

The beautiful spring light,
The magnificent colors of
Renewal
I cannot live in the
Shadow of my failing
Heart.
I want to drink in
The rich fragrance of
Summer, just peeking over
The horizon of this
Year of endings.

6.14.18

Strolling Away

Wish I could march
Away from my dying
Body.
If the body has a
Season mine is in
Late autumn.
Can you hear the
Crackle of leaves,
Smell the smoke
Of wood fires?
Can you remember
Her for who she is
Balancing between
Life and disappearance,
Excavating the wind-swept
Waves from
Which she first emerged?

6.22.18

Passage

You cannot remember but
Know, inside where blood
Leaves a trail through
Your terrain, that you
Were alone in the
Deconstruction.
You know that, even
With frantic help, your
Soul had won its
Fight with disappearance.
You were waving from
The storm of drowning,
You were calling to
Your dying heart:
Let's walk the rainbow
World once again, together.

Suddenly loss turned to
Mist and you could breathe
Without fear.

6.23.18

Found

What are the details of
Being kept alive?
Each moment a stranger
Coaxing, pleading
And flesh feeling a sensation
Of flesh.
You are apparent but you are
Gone.
The voices, the
Touch indistinguishable from
Body to spirit.
You are absent, you
Are walking a road of
The past, you are fighting
Like hell to reappear, feel
The sensation of another,
Feel alive in the black tunnel.
But life has waned-
You are keeping track
Of shooting stars, you are
Ablaze in a world without
End.
You see yourself
becoming indistinct amid a
vast stream of battling constellations…
You no longer need to
Walk among the souls of
The here and now,
You feel magnificent and free
Staring into the face of
Eternity.
You are so far away
You have met
Your first breath.

6.26.18

No Way Home

How does one return from
An electrical storm of strong
Winds and bolts of earth
Shaking lightening?
How does one return from
Death, then life and then
Death all over again?
It only lasts for a moment,
But it takes years of
Consciousness away.
Is life a temple?
Is life a mirage?
Is life bleeding onto the
Ground or blending into
The soul?
 When I knocked on the
Door of awakening
Did I leave one foot
In the darkness?

6.29.18

That Other Self

I know I stepped off
A cliff and lived to tell.
I can still feel the
Free fall, the fear of
Crashing, the rush of starlight.
I don't understand my
Return from strange
Trespass…
But I was carved out
Of my original flesh,
Drugged, jolted. And then
An opening was created.
I couldn't breathe, I
Couldn't see, I did not
Know my name.
I came back out of the darkness
To bare witness to
Someone I no longer am, and to
A world I can no longer
Love.

6.29-30.18

The Reveal

I will not last,
I will not meet
The oncoming years
On this earth-turning
Voyage.
Already the energy of
Life, the force of life, parts
Ways with my opened arms.
I have no regrets
For I have already seen
The beauty and drama of
The world. I have made my
Way over miles of
Roads and many years of
Joy, longing and disruption.
I will not last, my mind,
I am bound for a
World without borders,
A sky without gravity,
A spirit without this life.
Time stops us all.
Time cannot be measured
By a human
Being. Time is an elusive
Promise. A promise always
Unraveling.

7.1.18

Last Prayer

The exit, the way
The wind will carry you,
The way you will be
Taken from here
Forever
All of us,
Gone, and forgiven.

7.10.18

Retreating

Maybe you will remember
That I was once here,
Once alive,
And that I left
Way before I
Died.

7.10.18

Points of Light

It only takes one breezy
Moment to lose the thread
And tumble into freefall.
It only takes one uneven
Heartbeat to throw you into
Chaos.
I did not leave my life
In limbo, not a chance
I could still breathe
If I had.
The heart is a reckless
Warrior.
Life, life, life above all
Else, doesn't recognize death
Calling.
You stake your mind on
Continuous breath and only
Then do you take the dive.

7.14.18

What is Left

Now that life
Is in the process of giving
Up the ghost we have
Dreams of the odyssey…
What really happened
That night in the dark December
Dead zone?
Her body & soul were
Turned inside out
And given over to
The roar of eternity.
She cannot repeat that
Journey any more than
She can recall who she
Was without oxygen.
She knows so well, even
In blindness, that the body
And the mind were
Held hostage by the
Hateful drug of suffocation,
The strange ocean that
Cascades into reckless, breathless
Blackout.
There are no dreams left
When you are delivered
To the shoreline; a broken, bewildered
Bundle of loss.
You can no longer hear
The soaring, touching song
That was once lifeblood.
All has stopped, all is silent,
All has been left
Imprisoned in the tides
As they drift, drift, drift without
Thought or time or end.

7.15.18

Saved?

My body held hostage
On the death bed,
While my soul leaps
The boundaries.
Catch me if you can…

7.23.18

Sleep Walker

I am very aware that many
People are spooked by my
Survival. People are afraid of
Those who've lived
To tell.
I am very aware that I am a
 A mirage.
"Where did she go?" they ask.
."I used to Know her" they whisper quietly.
But it is their fear and my painful
Slide as I make me way back.

Who is the stranger?

7.31.18

Liftoff

Would I have welcomed
The return if I had
Known how diminished
My life would be?
The body and mind fight
Like a kind of madness,
To surface…
To surface…
But the spirit?
I will rock this damaged
self to sleep, with the
Help of my singed soul,
And the great roar from
Distant stars.

I am almost home again.

8.3.18

The Pageant

Time hurries away. But
Where does it land?
Is time still ringing
The bells of 17th century
Churches?
Is time sullen as it drains
The world of knowledgeable
Men & woman in silent
Contemplation?
Is time a priest creating
Portraits for eternity?
Time misses a step or falls
Asleep and those who believe
Time is poetry
Continue to write, paint and die.

8.13.18

Launch

The body fights against death
Even when the mind
Is absorbed in living.
The body cannot believe in
Death. *Not yet, not yet…*
While the mind opens
The sea shell where consciousness
Began.

8.19.18

Seeing

Here comes the wind
Again
And I'm not on the
Precipice.
I have moved the
Tarot card so that it can
No longer be placed
In a deadly prediction.

8.20.18

Rip-Tide Moon

It was the sea once,
Where I kept my
Transcendence,
Where I discovered
Freedom winged its way
Along the shore,
Where I discovered
That life does not end
But keeps flowing as
The currents drive the
Light and darkness,
Each breath and cry.
Life does not end
It vanishes into the surface
Of the awakening sea,
The beauty and wonder
Of the final flight, as it
Disappears into the unsettled
Voice of the tides.

9.6.18

The Circle Opens

I cannot see what you
Are doing nor where you
Have gone.
There is no definition to
Your face, body, dreams.
I cannot remember who
You were when you dipped
In to the abyss, where it
Has taken you.
Near death is stream-of
Consciousness, a jet stream
All along the imaginary sea.
You dive into the circle but
Are haunted by your missing
Soul. You dive, yes, and
Breathe, mostly, and you feel
Pain, when awake, yes.
So, this is the door
Opening. This is the
Page turning,
This is what is
Above you without a name
Or a clear path to
The next moment.
I dove. I whispered, I felt
That I was missing even
Though I could feel how
Deeply the spirit
Could go.
You can take me, yes,
But I can bow down
To life, and live on, live on.

9.18.18

Launching Again

It is not yet winter
And yet I have come
In from a world of
Dark hallucinations &
Psychic pain.
The body and its cells
Remember inspite of
The mind being untethered.
I rode many miles,
Unconscious, but awake
To my roller coaster in
Starlight, knowing
It was only a matter of time
For the descent to
Open into darkness &
Light, and the world
Unknown but touchable.
You cannot drift long
And still be sailing on
The surface.
I arose from the
Ruins, blacklisted from
My life. I can now
Hear, clearer than ever
Before, the rush of
Voices & emotions as
They carry me to a
New, unexplored land,
Alone.

9.23.18

Walking The Path

You will know I have
Returned again when you
Know I have come
From a long, dim & harrowing
Distance.
I can sit quietly now that
The trail of blood has passed
Many miles of barren
Landscape.
I arrive as I am
Released…
Even the days that
Ended brought anticipation of hallucination.

Darkness must reinvent
Itself in the image of
An awakening ghost.

9.27.18

Here Now

It will be a day to
 remember because
it is a day that has
passed.
So, what does a small
pocket of time surrender?
Do the minutes mesh into a
landscape of change,
erosion, decay?
It will be a day to
remember, yes
and it will be lives
who have passed, not just time…
Don't wait, walk
with purpose, the
horizon is losing its
light.

10.1.18

The Mood of Endings

I have nothing more to
Give in the early October
Dance. The leaves twirl
Around on the dying lawn,
The lights come on earlier.
The road where our lives
Are lived grows chilly and
Barren.
I no longer close my eyes
Where the past breaks in, full of sentiment.
These seasons of turning darkly
Are upon us. The voices of
Children are calling in the
Distance, people close
Doors and stand in windows,
Waiting.
What is it that the
Colorful dead leaves bring?
Only to memorialize the
Days
Taken. Taken…
The orange fields of
Pumpkins, the cold breeze,
Apple cider, long gone, the
Ghosts who used to
Live here.
My mind is beginning to
Rest. Soon sleep will
Usher in the twists &
Turns of the earth spinning
Endlessly toward god.
There is no way out
As Autumn seals
Us into lives of
Longing, of loss.
My shadow clambering
In the hills, expressing
All of the life gone
Stale and helpless.

Love is gathering the lost
Ones. They never left,
They never return.
Do you hear the quiet
Storm of voices, calling? They are
Whispering, *there is nothing more*
To give."

10.7.18

Vanishing Point

I could not talk to my
Body as it went into twilight,
As day & night and
Luminous stars made their
Circuitous rounds, and the
Body slept.
How can you sleep with a
War erupting inside the
Comatose self?
How can you remain
So still
While the earth of
The body is struggling
To rise above the rubble?
You no longer reside in
Calm repose as an
Earthquake dismantles your
Soul?
When morning turns,
And turns again
You are lying in
The battlefield and your
Blood awakens.
In the east the sky is ablaze
But you are
Paralyzed. Is it heaven?

11.8.18

Whiplash

She was busy trying to shake the
Ghost out of her rib cage.
She was not comatose
She was in some new
Playground, unemotional, cold.
There was no movement
And yet the air held
Many floating, many floating…mysteries.
When morning arrived
She still didn't stir, she
Did not ask for light or
Food.
You can trace her last
Look into the break of
Day. She is diving. She is not drowning.
She no longer wants to surrender.
She is the final breath.

11.14.18

The Scope of Endings

Absolution in the form of
The laboring heart. If you
Are saved, are you filled
With god?
Now I lay Me Down...
The spirit blasted out of
The way and the dying
Body took notice.
Absolution and the
Sky opened.
How does one measure
The resumption of deep breath and the energy of
Blood flow, circling, a
Return?
I saw what it took to
Surface, all of my past
Helping me reach for
The lighted ascension. From
The deep place. The retreating soul
And then you rise
And are fully awake.
It is spring. Snow, your
Buriel dissolves in
Sunlight.
You remember
Everything. Nothing has
Been left to die. You
Remember, and the
Day unfolds again and
Again, you focus your truth
On the movement
Of minutes with your blindness
Along for the last ride out.

11.18.18

Path From Home

The one and only home
Is the one you dream
From.
As a girl my light flickered
Through the coastal
Neighborhoods, sometimes
Singing to myself, sometimes
On alert as the sea breeze
Brought nightfall.
The schoolyard wire fence,
The bike ride through
Narrow, foggy streets.
I remember alleyways,
I remember boozed up
Mothers and fathers.
Did they ever sit quietly
Succumbing softly to the flameless hours
As they roared by?
I would twirl on the
Lawn in the front yard.
At night nothing happened
But we lived in fear.
I become dizzy thinking of
What was relinquished, what has
Never been retrieved
In semi-conscious apprehensions.
The passing, an
Endless dance on alert.
What brought me to the
Everywheres I never
Inhabited long?
There were, I swear,
Always miracles, always
New thoughts—and music
Of The Beatles…so new
We were driven to hysterical
Thrills. And sadness, longing.
All of it packed away, not
Forgotten, not passing into

Dust.
I remember so well the
Warmth of my best friends
House. We played school.
We listened to music, and
Her parents hovering but
Distant, drinking their cocktails.
The picture you paint, dear memory, is of sea &
Sand dunes, swing sets, salty
Feet, the deaths, the deaths…
I was alive, we were alive
But we were ghosts. All of us living
Through a dark pattern of hours. We
Didn't inhabit the
BBQ parties in the backyard,
We lie on the lounge
Chairs watching night slowly
Move over us.
I remember, I remember
The feeling that it would
Never end and yet
Change was constantly
On a sailboat, taking us
To another land where we could never live.

11.1.18

Reawakened

Do we begin in the past
With no memory, no history,
Only to begin?
Is sleep the charge of
Life?
You must rummage through an
Energy-moving wave,
You must survive to
See the light in your eyes
Dancing in the distance.
Suddenly you are moving into
Suffocating territory— a black
Hole where creation trampled darkness.
Again and again you recall the
Mad dash of travelling time
Your mind made up of
Sparks of surfaces moving
Beyond the displacement of the soul.

11.1.18

Moored Nowhere

They do not know how
Quickly the sun can set.
They do not recognize
How quickly the mind can
Vanish into chaos… or
How life can dissolve
Away.
You've lost the dream of an abundance
Of time,
You've lost the path to the stars.
What you have gained
Is a last vision, and
A firey collision.
Do you see yourself
Out-bound?
Have you fed your
Life into the void,
Where no one arrives, and therefore
No one is lost?

11.17.18

The Light Dreams On

I could hear the birds
Speaking, the voices said
"Stay with Us, We heal you,
You can fly"
The wind spoke—poetry.
I could hear the lakes,
Their calm words
Of joy, reflection of
The infinite.
The messages around me,
The holy fragrance,
The deep settling of the
Heavens.
I remember I could feel
The tremble of
The new frontier.
When I began to die,
Guided by the peace of
Prayer: *go back, go back.*
I am listening as I dream.
And my name, our names
Are embedded in the world.

2.3.19

Fortune

If it were any darker
We'd be covered in stars

2.15.19

Passing

My heart was only
Toxic for the short run, was only awake in the
Deep end.
All eyes watching
Whisked away, the mind
As ghost.
Sleeping through calamity.
Why do images from my
Past wander through, as if
I am still living there,
But not then.
My body screams while
The mind naps…unaware, unaware,
Unaware.
The electric spark of
Consciousness
Being written from
Another age.
You are lucky to have
Starved the graveyard, settled
In intoxicating air.
When you lose the race
You feel nothing, but you
Must be alive to retreat into
Solitary.
Go now, said the
Empty sky
Go now says the heart.

3.9.19

Staircase

It was on the border
Where I parted ways with
My soul. I met you there.
The swaying trees,
The tearful sky,
The long path to the
Top of the receding world.
It was freefall on the
Border,
No doorway back to life.
God no longer rings true
But I remember, I remember
Believing.
So far away from grace and yet my
Heart felt safe.
Did love remain?

Does life hold me tightly as we
leap into history?

3.24.19

The Path at Last

When a star explodes
Consciousness begins.
The awakening stream is
Not darkness.
The immense light-vanished
Trail was enveloped into
The body.
The soul interprets the
Sun shining inside a precise outline of
Shadows within.
When I stepped off the
Train in a silent
Forbidding street
I did not die.
Only the future knows
How far I've yet to go.

3.24.19

Intruding

It is dark, not because
There is no moon, or the
Branches of the skeletal winter
Trees are blowing.
No, it is dark because so
Much of my life was left
In the emergency room.
The doors closed on
Mind. The ticking away of time.
It is dark because you
Succumbed to death, several
Times, the fall into, the resuscitation.
Not once did they imagine
What I had become, not once
Could they imagine what I
Left when I lost the dream of
Self.
Gone is nowhere, it is not a
Toxin to be evaluated.
Gone is so deeply black.
So deeply a massacre that
Cannot be calculated.
My fingers brushed the edge
As they passed the
Bottom, the end
In sight.
It is dark, not because
All light is gone
But because freedom
Has no outline. Freedom reaches
Back for the
Heart
And the heart leans toward
Peace in a world overwhelmed
By fear.

4.2.19

I'm Here

There was violence from
The stranger
Who tried to awaken
The heart.
The soul plunged for a
Split second
And then resumed its flutter in the
Embrace of fog.

4.7.19

Uneven Path

I spend so much time trying
To nudge my spirit to wake up.
I have been there, watching my
Life stumble by in the winter
Trees.
You have no idea who you
Are when you become a
Fragmented whole.
Does our survival matter?
We imagine life travelling
Down the skyway
With no turning point or point
Of reference.
I gave my soul back to the
Horizon from which it came.
Night no longer answers, it
Relinquishes.

1.28.19

Remaining Present

There is a sense that
Something is coming to
A close
But the magnificent shadows do not
Reflect that.
I imagine spring as a
Symptom of having
Survived. Survival,
Even just the word, sounds
Like a long difficult, dust borne journey.
I stepped away for a
Time. What stirred inside
Me were only the mechanics
Of having felt.
The route of blood, a barely audible
Voice all its own.
Water, salt, iron
Build a life.
But, it is worth surrendering as
It charges up the flesh?
There was once a pattern
Here: concrete, powerful,
A reflection of the energy
Of time————in motion.
When the silence comes
With warm flesh
You will dawn as ghost
But stasis will
Be the sense all around
You.
A blessing has carried you
And you are astonished
As the path drinks you in—and frees you.

5.7.19

The Ghost Travels

I did not belong in
My own body. I was
Not alive in my own flesh.
Blood is a train that
Cannot forgo everlasting.
The machines held court.
I was no longer…
I was no longer
Sailing. I was shipwrecked.
The land fell
The sky, suffocating sky…
I did not memorize
The light, extinguished.
It was not night, but
The beginning
Of a vision
Outside of
Consciousness, evaporating and expanding.
The mind no longer
Spoke.
Language succumbed and receded into
The flow of time.
I did not come close
To waking.
I did not come close
To the final commemoration,
Paving the way
to starlight.

6.10.19

The Moment of Faith in Freefall

It was in the land
Of the caretakers.
She did not awaken to
This new frontier. So many
Have abandoned life,
And they do not leave
Trails.
One summer we could
Smell the eucalyptus
Trees in the neighbor's yard.
We could swing on the swing sets
And look to the heavens, searching for
Peace in the sky.
I cannot possibly tell you
My feelings that day.
We were on the balcony
When we heard that
Marilyn had died. She had lived
In her small, dark room for
Many months.
Our lives changed. Youth
Has a straight line, from
The first thread of consciousness to
The noisy parade.
I used to imagine, if I could
Twirl fast enough
I would end up in the
Center of life.
Then I would walk six
Blocks to the beach. The
World opened, hope was
Awakening in my heart.
Navigating the waves, I
Believed in god.

7.1.19

Underneath, and Diving

It was the loneliness I remember
Most. To travel alone into deep
Self, let loose in a replenished universe
Starving for oxygen and light.
Twirling into a long, narrow, star-filled
Tunnel, with no way back.
The puzzle of infinity
Was eclipsed by the pull
Of stability.
How long did the journey
Last—in circles, no
Balance, no help, no one.
When did the dizziness die
Down?
When did the soul reverse
The energy long enough to hale
A magnificent understanding in
Stillness, breathing hard as after
A marathon. The body lands
In disorientation. Disorientation
Becomes liberation.

7.5.19

To the Shoreline

We continue to walk those
Hills, our tennis shoes
Flying over concrete.
We knew we were pursuing
The shoreline, the warm sand,
A sky full of sea spray.
We continue to smell the
Red tide & feel the soft
Curves of beached seaweed &
Shell fragments.
The dreaming that took us
To last light in a soft
Breeze beginning its evening
Mist.
We could have died
There. There was only one
Season on the beach.
The season of salt water air,
Golden sun dropping into dark
Breaking waves & the
Diving and screaming of
Gulls.
I spent my childhood
Twirling beneath the sky.

7.22.19

Found, Again

Pretend like you are going
To start over. Erase that
Fateful day, those dreams
Of childhood, your mother
Passed out on the couch with
A cigarette burning through her
Night gown.
Erase the sound of the
Sea, the tides rolling in,
The rising sun. Voices
Of children running down the
Strand toward the pier.
Pretend like you are going
To start over. But, you cannot
Rid yourself of the past, you
Cannot creep into the skin of a new
Starting point.
Well said, said the god of welcome.
You will always be home.

10.8.19

Meeting the Tides

It was as if I were
Living in a country, displaced.
Push on, move on, your
Soul is not masquerading among the
Trees, or shadowed by the
Moon's light.
It was being taken
Away, it was dizzy
Spinning as the impending night
Waited…
I knew I would rendezvous
With that other sky, that world
Of enchantment.
The machines kept their
Distance as the days passed,
When I was mute & blind.
She was meant to leave
No trace but the shoreline
Was astonished by the radiance of the
Seashells she had gathered.

10.13.19

Bleeding

It was an appointment kept.
But the evening started so
Innocently and peacefully.
Who knew the dragon was
Descending? I could not
Read it along the line of setting
Sun. I could not fend
Against the pull of a new
Perilous year. Was the drum
Sounding in the quiet winter
Eruption?
I sensed my disappearance
Not the tearing, the severing.

10.15.19

Left

If I could speak from
That speck of self.
If I could *describe the
Lost one, the lost one...*
But she was shaken from
Her steady planking. Her
Eyes reverted to paralysis...
Her heart, her heart
Traveled so far from its
Fiery center.
If I could speak from
That vanished self
I would say it is nothing.
No worries, flying from the
Pulsating body to a new
World, an unexplored
World.
Who knows how it ends?
You return and you are again
The dream.
You feel the missing
Pieces of self, a startling energy.
Why did I embark
On this journey? Taken
From my body, banished
From my life.
It is all an essence
Beyond sky. It is all
An essence, miles high.
You will know when it's
Time to die.

10.26.19

Tish Pearlman is a poet, writer, broadcast journalist and community and political activist originally from Manhattan Beach, California. For 15 years she was host of the award-winning arts/public affairs public radio interview show "Out of Bounds." www.outofboundsradioshow.com

In the 1970's and 80's Pearlman was actively writing and gave many readings at political and literary events on the central California coast. Her work also appeared in many literary journals and magazines including *Street Cries, Adventures in Poetry Anthology, Carousel Quarterly,* and *Latitude/20*. She began to write poetry again in 2009. Her current work has appeared in *The Healing Muse Literary Journal* (2010-2022), *The Ithaca Times, The Syracuse Post-Dispatch Healthy CNY Magazine, Conversations Across Borders Literary Magazine, Earth's Daughters* and *The Iconoclast Literary Journal*. One of her poems was accepted for publication in an anthology titled *The Art of Medicine in Metaphors*, published in January 2013.

Her collection, re-telling her near-death heart surgery experience, is a chapbook entitled *The Fix Is In* and was published by Finishing Line Press in January 2012.

Her full-length collection *Afterlife* was published by Foothills Publishers in May 2014.

She was the 2013 & 2014 Poet Laureate of Tompkins County, NY.

www.ingramcontent.com/pod-product-compliance
Lightning Source LLC
Chambersburg PA
CBHW042130160426
43198CB00022B/2972